# Golden Inspirations through Poetry

### Written by

## Bernice Golden

### Compiled by

### Sallie L. Moppert

ISBN: 1517497531
ISBN-13: 978-1517497538

i

## DEDICATION

I would like to dedicate this book to all of my family, faithful followers and friends, who have stood by me for years. Many of them have been in need of one thing or another. I will always be there for them, just as I have in the past. But I want to thank each and every one of you for all the love and prayers you have given me throughout the years.

A special thank you goes to ReusableArt.com for the images used in this book.

# TABLE OF CONTENTS

## A Friend

To be stern when expected

    To be close when in need

To expect no returns

    For each and every deed.


To hear all complaints

    With no judgments to pass

To reach out a hand

    With a love that will last.


To give what can be given

    Whether in spirit or mind

Is that of a true friend

    And thank God, you're mine.

## <u>People</u>

I know many people who are sly as a fox,

But many as gentle as lambs

Yet others are stubborn as brahma bulls

and more often act like rams.

There are many who roar like a lion

and others are meek as cats.

There are some who are devious as a snake

and others I'd consider rats.

## The Bond of Friendship

Tears no longer cloud your eyes
For I've come to keep them dry
With love and compassion on those dreary days
When you feel the urge to cry.

Pass not through this world alone
Fret not for I am near
To help mend your wounded heart
And to cleanse away your tears.

The heart may be burdened from time to time,
With worries beyond control.
But remember the bond of friendship we have
So we may reach our attainable goals.

## If I Only Had But One Moment

If I only had but one moment
to spend with you in this life
I would stop the world from spinning
at a time when there is no strife

I would capture the happiest moment
that we shared in warmth as one
With your face beaming lovingly
desire showing bright as the sun.

## What is Love?

To love is to accept

       To love is to give

To love is to care

       To love is to live

To expect no returns

       To expect no gains

To expect no rewards

       Is a love that remains

## Who is God?

A feeling of knowing
that someone stands by
A sense of direction
and not asking why.

A strength with love
punishment with caring
Trusting with love
compassion with sharing.

Accepted wisdom and spirit
of a force without a nod
Of a superior being
we know of as God.

## To My Family

A special gift that no monies could buy
was a thought I wanted to share.
To give love and feelings from my heart
To my family who really cares.

I don't often say "I love you, dad."
But you're always here in my heart.
No matter whatever step between
or the miles that keep up apart.

To both my dear brothers whom lest often I see
You're both very much part of my life
For as the years continue to fly
There will only be love not strife.

With even a "sister," not an "in law"
with a child who is now my niece
I love all of you more than you'll ever know
and wish love, contentment and peace.

# Life's Journey

As a creator with the hands of a master
Each board is placed with care
Each sail is woven with the finest thread
To withstand the turbulent wear

As it is pushed into the water's edge
The waves peak with a boisterous sound
Echoing words of a new journey's birth
Not knowing where it's abound

As the sails are set for the travel to start
The skies are blue and white
To anticipate the stormy days
Would be conceding to a fight

For this ship has been built with the deepest of love
To withstand the harsh blowing gales
To stand firm and tall with wondrous pride
Til its hull becomes utterly frail

She must not weaken 'gainst the mighty storms
On the seas rolling waves so high
For she has her duties to complete in time
With the love of her master's eye

The winds may blow and the rains may fall
Never knowing where lightening may strike
With a vicious roar and a bellowing sound
And no two being ever alike

The sails may weather and few tears may show
As she nears her journey's end
To approach again where she was built
Where she knows her master as friend

## Bear Not the Witness of Hate

Do no harbor the feelings of contempt
Bear not the witness of hate
Cast off the shadows of darkness
And the wishings of ill-fate.


For the knowledge of God is not hidden
Seek ye the words of love
For the meek and humble of God
Flows free as the wings of a dove.


Sit on these wings and glide
Fear not the journeys of life
For all that is needed to succeed
Will be given in love, not strife.

## To Know

To know is really not know,
For all known cannot be.
For all that is to be known,
Is more than the eye can see.

To have faith without knowledge,
And belief without seeing,
To love without receiving,
Is to be the total being.

All the knowledge of being,
And all the laws of God,
Are to be accepted as given,
And used in the paths we trod.

## The Grand Ole Opry

Under this roof and within these walls,

There's an echo of true emotions.

From the heartiest of laughter to ease one's soul

And heartaches with no solution.


She has seen the banjos break many strings,

And a sour notes once in a while,

But she holds her honor firm and strong

And just stares back with a smile.


There's been many she's helped when really in need,

To open the doors of success.

She's held their hand and wiped their brow,

Knowing they've really given their best.


She knows it's not just showmanship

That will keep their legends strong,

But the love that all have given

With a feeling to belong.

She's not just a structure built by man
For a profit alone to see,
But the breath and life of many a soul
God bless The Grand Ole Opry.

### Life?

What is the essence of life

Can you give me the proper proportions

I'd like to mix ten gallons

and pass it out as lotion.

# A Puzzle

Life is but a puzzle
Criss-crossing every way
Finding words with definitions
Throughout each and every day

With the struggles of life
and their mingling ways
I thought life was crosswords
But found it a maze

I searched for the answers
That would fit each phrase
Found only conclusion
and half deafened with craze

Though with a pen in my hand
I so graciously write
Give me the answers
and turn on the light

## Accept Me

I need the time to be free as the wind
Sweeping softly through the trees,
Facing storms and currents of life's times
But still flowing with the breeze

If you heed not my warning to walk away
Stay close, but not behind
Do not drain me of strength or integrity
Do not play silly games with my mind.

Allow me to care with a free flowing love
With an understanding of what I must do.
For I am still an adventurer in this world today
Searching for the answers that are new.

Accept me as you would the seas
With the waters flowing rapidly by
Try not to build an enormous dam
For I know I would surely die

Hold not the reigns of love too tight

Hang them loose so that I may lead

The life of a wandering drifter

To those who are in need.


For there may be a day when you'll know what I mean

And there'll be no questions to ask.

You'll accept me for what I truly am

And face life without a task.

## Praise to the Thinker

Make way for the thinker
for there are few to find
Most people enjoy resting
instead of using their mind.

Praise him with believing
to help him succeed
for he needs your support
to continue his lead.

Look to the future
he holds in his hands.
This could be yours with strength to demand.

## Unquestionable Love

Looking through and beyond
those soft billowy clouds
Lies a world where love flows free
with a whisper of warmth from God's loving breath
and a knowing of who he must be.

For I know there's a somewhere
much more peaceful than this
where God's opened love shows bright
with an understanding of human mistakes
where no darkness appears, just light.

The clouds will open and a smile appears
on our gracious master's face.
For he knows we're truly his creation of time
and will help us with no disgrace.

For we're molded of flesh with emotions to bear
on this world of forbidden time.
With the burdens and worries and paths to choose
never knowing which one to leave behind.

For the choice of believing has been given to us
with guidance from only above.
Where the clouds have opened and a smile appears
and we accept with an unquestionable love.

For his love is pure and no questions he asks.

## Marriage of the Heart

The doubt, the worries, the concerns
of truth to this birth of love
Is beyond the doors of reality
Or does it come from above?

For I've been so alone for so many years
Independence of my own is my life
and no one to share my emotions with
whether in love, hatred, or strife

I'm afraid to trust with an open heart
for I want no more hurt and pain
Yet I feel myself drawing closer to you
and thinking of trying again.

There's a feeling I can't begin to explain
changing the many thoughts of my heart
wanting you with me as much as we dare
and not wanting to be apart.

You've unlocked a hidden emotion
in this lonely world of mine.
An emotion of sincere ecstasy
that I never thought I'd find.

I feel so secure and safe
while nestled in your arms
the worries and cares of the world
could never be a harm

For I know you would protect me
as best you know you could
and truly care beyond all words
The way a lover should.

I'll demand not a thing of you
other than honesty and caring
and a shoulder to cry on when needed
with a feeling of truly sharing.

Marriage of the heart is more important
than any contract could ever be
Just knowing we're tied in heart as one
means all the world to me.

We both belong to others
with commitments we both must keep
and by breaking them we both would lose
respect that runs ever so deep.

I'll remain yours for as long as you want
with sincerity and devoted trust.

## A Woman

A woman's a woman
       No matter what's said,
With long flowing hair
       And no shaven head.


With rounded bosoms
       And no chest hair to show,
I'm a woman, indeed,
       With a radiant glow.


I like my doors opened,
       My cigarettes lit.
I enjoy my soft body,
       That's not muscularly fit.


I like pretty makeup
       With various hues
       And luscious lipstick
       And glittering rouge.

I'm proud I'm a female,

     Making love to a man.

Even though this seems crazy,

     I don't give a damn.


Be who you are

     And what God made you to be.

You'll be a happier person,

     Just wait and see.

## Mother to Child

As the womb grows very heavy
     And a new life begins to appear
With these words of love I greet you
     To this new world of love, my dear.


As a new beautiful creation in body
     But of a spirit of old that you are
The love that we both shall attain
     Is something that will never be marred.


To watch the growth of spirit and body
     To see your face glimmer with glee
Just to know that I'm your mother
     Means more than the world to me.

## What Do You See?

Look in the mirror
and what do you see?
Are you one of those thinkers
or just pretend to be?

Why waste your life
or would you rather do so.
It's totally up to you,
But I'd rather say no.

For I'm a believer
in controlling our life.
I'd rather be happy
than live in strife.

## Your Life's Diary

Just think of yourself as a book on the shelf
with a thousand pages of life
with each chapter a part of your being
showing love, and strength and strife.

Each chapter's a section of a new beginning,
Trying to forget what's already past,
yet having to remember each word that's been
written
so you'll understand to the last.

But how many forget the chapters they've read?
Do you really think they'll remember your name?
Or will you get dusting and your binding stay new
behind those who have reached fame.

## Wonder

Could we be sleeping somewhere else
in another dimension of time
Could we really be living a dream each day
in the subconscious part of a mind

Who is to say we're not somewhere else
where time's not equal to ours
where one full lifetime here on earth
Somewhere else could be just an hour

Maybe they've ahead of us
Or maybe just behind.
Who really has the answers
I know they're hard to find.

## Belief

On Easter Eve, the skies were gray.
The wind whirled round and round.
The trees whistled beautiful songs.
And the rain poured steadily to the ground.

As I sit close to my window
I pondered thoughts of years ago
and wondered if Christ was our savior
so we could really learn to grow.

Was he crucified as the bible said
with spikes driven through his hands and
was he ruthlessly put upon that cross
with thorns on his head as a band

Did he shed his blood to save our sins
with torture beyond our thoughts
Did he forgive those who induced the pain
no matter how hard they fought?

Was he a man or just a myth
with a legend to carry us though
Is he a spirit that surrounds us all
with words that are warm and true

Is he really love and compassion
with answers to all mankind
Should we really follow his encouraging words
for then, what shall we really find

Will we find peace and wisdom of mind?
Will we find contentment with trust?
Will we learn to grow up spiritually
and find this world unjust?

What are the answers, I asked the clouds
as they hastily drifted by
If he really was such a terrific man
Then why did he have to die?

As I uttered these words, the rain abruptly stopped
The skies suddenly shown bright above
A voice from beyond began to speak
with words, "I Am Truly Love."

"Yes I died to make man holy.
Yes I died to set man free.
Yes I shed my blood for all mankind.
Yes, I am Christ, now can't you see?"

"Push aside your disbelief.
Make time for the righteous way
Heed close to the words of the holy book
for you'll see me again someday."

As his voice began to fade away
and the skies returned to gray,
I realized that my doubts weren't true
and no more will I feel dismay.

For this voice in the mighty beyond

Gave me reason to truly conceive

That that's really a God somewhere up above

If we're strong enough to believe.

## True Love

As the flowers bloom in the spring
so shall my love for you
With the petals opening by the morning light
showing the vibrant lustrous hues

With the dew glistening in the sun's warming rays
on the crisp morning of love's birth,
I stand in the window of happiness
covered with the scent of myrrh

I'm waiting to see your glowing face
after a night on our bed of love
just to hear you whisper "good morning, dear"
as I thank the Lord up above

I never knew the meaning of love
'til I entered as one with you
As your friend and lover of all times
my life suddenly had different views

For now I feel like I'm a person
with a reason to keep on living
I will share my total being
and take not, but just keep giving

For I want to give all that I can
to keep the flowers blooming
I know that I truly love you
and that I'm not just assuming

## Open Your Heart

Bring me your worries and all your fears
let me hold you close in my arms.
For the hurt I feel from your trembling heart
no more will feel love's harm.


Lay your head up on my shoulder
and weep til the morning is nigh
Listen to your beating heart
with echoes of a love gone by.


Throw away the emotions as a onetime fool
awaken to a new morning light
Conquer a new path in the honor of love
and never concede to a fight.


For a true love will be given
as sure as the sun shines above
Cleanse your soul and open your heart
Let it fly to you from the angels above.

## What You Show

Tell me you love me, tell me you care
Don't assume I already know
For a woman needs attentiveness
No matter where she goes

Fear of affections and wanting to show
others how much you care
Will only lead to destruction
to the one that you really care

If you're ashamed for others to know
how you really feel about me
Then toss aside our relationship
and pronounce yourself as free

## Inside I Weep

Doing right what's supposed to be wrong
is all I want to do.
Stealing a moment whenever we can
just sharing my dreams with you.

Someone else's ring is on your hand
but my love is within your heart.
Even though in another's bed you sleep
our souls will never part.

Our love is a bond of endless time
with a depth n'er to be known
with a surge of passion running through our veins
even when we stand alone.

My mind will often drift beyond
with hazed images of you
Making love to someone else
and wondering if you knew

That I've been thinking how you feel
knowing I'm alone
Waiting for your words of love
if only by the phone.

For I'll always be the other one
whose love you chose to keep
with no commitments or wedding bands
even though inside I weep.

But these tears are not just loneliness
for you, my only love
But tears to make a rainbow path
with the sun when we meet above.

## It's the Point of View

Is the pond deep or shallow

Is the tree thick or hollow

Is the grass short or long

Are the birds singing a song


Is the sky blue or gray

Is it August or the middle of May

Are the clouds white or black

What's the difference from front to back?

## Not Just a Haunting Memory

You're not just a haunting memory
Still bringing tears to my eyes
After all these years I've not let go
Nor could I say goodbye.

I've not loved anyone as I have you
even though it's been fifty years
No one could ever take your place
To help me through the years

As my hair is white and my legs are weak
I still find the love to be strong
With a burning desire of passion and warmth
and a wanting to belong

My days are short before I leave
this earth with its suffering and pain
I'll soon be there by your side
and I'll hurry with no refrain.

For no one has ever taken your place

No matter whatever it would be

You're still the only part of my heart

and not just a haunting memory.

## Humanity

As I live in the world of disbelief
I travel through life alone
With shadows standing by my side
and hearts as cold as stone.


No trust have I for my fellow man
who astutely shows his greed
For he's a man of liar's tears
That shall never be truly free.


He can bind you to the worthless thoughts
with fears and lack of trust
His world is made of ruthlessness
and gold is but a must
His sharing is something rarely seen
except for he himself

## Return to the Scene of the Crime

I loved you more than life itself
with a desire to please you forever
Not once thinking you'd hurt me

You've been gone five long years
and suddenly returned
wanting me back with a strong desire
realizing the lessons you've learned

I died inside the day you left
to fall into the arms of another
You stood and watched my tears fall down

The day has come as I knew it would
Now you've returned without a dime
wanting me back to heal your heart
as you return to the scene of the crime

## So Shall I

As a tree grows from seed

To a long lengthy root

To a strong sturdy trunk

And branches with leaves

So shall I.


As the leaves open in spring

Change golden in fall

Seeds fall to the ground

To grow again with all

So shall I.

## To Care

As each day progresses
with the thought of you near
Makes me stronger in love
and lessens my fear

To know that you care
to know that you're mine
Gives me a true happiness
with a radiant smile

To envelope you in a favorable way
with a protection of love that is true
Proves total sincerity and honesty
with days that are no longer blue

## Fido

Look at the dog bury the bone

he found while out there all alone.

He hides it deep and hides it well,

not even his friends does he tell.


He leaves for a while so no one will know,

that his prize is hidden ever so low.

He plans to return when no one's around,

when everyone's gone and there's no sound.


The day finally comes when he plans his feast,

and struts to his treasure like a beast.

As he digs in frustration and finds nothing there,

his lesson of selfishness was taught by a hare.

## To Believe

With a melody of whispers,

The wind blows through.

The world and its mysteries

Are really not new.


We know not the true reason why.

But to believe and feel,

To have faith and love.

Will give us answers when the time is nigh.


To open one's heart,

To open one's mind,

Will give us direction

In what we're to find.


To follow the laws

That God has given,

Will bring closer the truth

For all that are living.

## Whither Thou Goest?

If you could travel far away
where do you think you would go?
Would you travel to the orient
on a ship going ever so slow?

Would you take time to travel to the island
set far in the ocean's ranges
or would you go straight up north
where the weather drastically changes?

Would you go to the highest Alps
to look down on the world below?
Would you take a camel to the deserts
where the sands can blindly blow?

Would you travel to see a lion's roar
or a python hanging from a tree
or a cathedral ringing chimes of time
or a pyramid that will always be?

Would you take the time to see the whales
jumping out of the water so high
or just look at the pretty sunset
graciously floating through the sky?

Wherever you go throughout the world,
remember how far you've come.
It matters not how far you go.
What counts is where you're from.

## The Wisdom of Innocence

I wonder if children should have been adults
and we be known as tots.
For sometimes their natural wisdom
is more often right than not.

Their meekness and humble response
to a warm loving kiss on the cheek
allows for a true relationship
which adults may forever seek.

Their honesty is above "superb."
Their wit is a fresh embrace
with an acceptance of one and others,
without having to hide their face.

They may argue with peers who are close
and may spat with those not known.
But, they're always the first to forget what's been
said
and give expressions of love that is shown.

## The Controller

Did you ever really look to the sky,

and wonder what lies beyond?

Where the stars glisten in the dark of the night,

and the moon is so big and round?


Could there be a controller pushing a button

on a panel so far away?

Controlling our lives and making us pay

for the errors we've made through the days?


Could we be but a puppet on a string,

attached to a star above,

With God making all the gestures,

but doing them all with love?

## Sitting Upon a Cloud

Can you imagine living upon a cloud
     with the rain falling down from below
With the trees reaching upward to greet you
     while you're comfortably drifting so low

Protected by your soft billowy cotton
     restful and warm as you are
Closer to God and his sunshine
     So close and yet so afar

The world with all of its concerns
     problems and cares so endowed
But please, don't be fretfully worried
     remember, you're sitting upon a cloud

## Please God, Take My Hand

As the hours grow close
      Where my new being begins
Understand that I need thee
      Though as human I've sinned.

To know where I've failed
      All the years that passed by
Will help me be stronger in spirit
      Though in body I die.

From where I have come
      I shall now return
To serve in your honor
      With more yet to learn

Accept my spirit as is
      My soul as I stand
Before thee I worship
      Now please, God, take my hand.

## Am I?

As free as the winds blow
>As soft as the clouds in the sky

As strong as the mighty oak
>So as my wish, Am I?


To accept what cannot be accepted
>To give without denying

To believe the unbelievable
>So as my wish, Am I?


To achieve the unachievable
>To live not in sin or lie

To care for the uncareable
>So as my wish, Am I?


To see strength in the weak
>To see rebirth, not die

To see love, not hatred
>So as my wish, Am I?

But to know my weaknesses

    In the days that go by

Give me the teachings and knowledge

    So as my wish, Am I!

## A Little Bit of Golden Wit

Look at the mouse running so fast

    See him scurry to hide in the grass

Or is it an elephant that I see not well

    Do you know the difference, or can't you tell?


Then look at the bird flying so high

    Or is it a saucer in the sky

Can you see if it's coming your way

    Or will it just fall and land in the hay?


But look to the mountain rising from the ground

    Or is it just an anthill not making a sound?

Is it big enough to climb to the top

    Or can you destroy it with one small hop?

## To a Lost Love

As I sit alone with each passing day
    My heart is heavy laden
With memories of a onetime love
    When I was your lovely maiden

I often wondered where you've traveled
    Or if you've matured in life
And if your hair is now silvery gray
    And your face withered with strife
We laughed and loved for so many years
    And caught glimpses of each other's past.
Yet, did we know that the day would come
    When our love would never last

To see ourselves five years ahead
    Seemed impossible for us to do
We knew that our love was eternally strong
    And planned forever to be true

When I noticed the restlessness as time went on

    And felt you were soon to leave

The knowing hurt within my heart

    Left me nothing, but to grieve


The day you turned and said goodbye,

    I couldn't fight the tears

For I knew I'd never see you again,

    But I'll always love you, my dear.

## To My Mother

Not all women can be a mother
>Even though that of child they can bear

It takes a special breed of woman
>With a true love and heart that cares.


A closeness when strife is breathing near
>A breath of sunshine when fear lurks close

Just a feeling of sincerity and strength
>Whenever you're needed in love the most.


No love is more binding, than that of a mother
>Whether close or so far apart

Just to know that she's mine in spirit and mind
>Will hold ever dear to my heart.

## My Father

As the years slip away
        And age begins to show
There is still the brilliance
        Of your wonderful glow.


The love that you've given
        The good that you've done
Gives all that are near you
        The warmth of the sun.


To show love and affection
        Even though you're a man
Makes me proud to be
        The child of yours that I am.

## Universal Sands

As a drifter in a world so minute,
As a grain in the universal sands,
I wash upon the shores of time
With only a minute in hand.

This moment in time that I have,
Is meant for the knowledge to gain,
To mature in my life as a spirit,
To reach a much higher plane.

To know why is not the questions,
The answer is but to survive,
To attain the Heavenly Kingdom
In the brief moment we have alive.

## My Salvation

Life has been a horror
of feelings beyond compare.
With twists and tangles of momentous strength
and worries I should not share.


What is happiness, I've asked myself,
with no answer for many years.
Til the door of salvation opened wide
and the love of God appeared.


Thankfulness was the furthest thought
from my weakened worldly mind.
Til I realized Christ had died for me
with a love I had to find.


The stumbling o'er the many rocks
of heartaches I've had to bear,
Are nothing but tiny pebbles
with the Lord at my side to share.

I've been asked how I can be thankful
when there's nothing going my way?
My answer to those who are blinded is,
"salvation is yours as you say,"

I accept Jesus as Lord and savior
as my father with no questions asked.
Obey his words from the Holy Book
and he'll carry you through your tasks.

Be thankful he died for your sins
and shed his blood with love for you
For the kingdom of God is yours to share
with a crown that is filled with jewels.

## My Sweetheart

To see what you are doing

To hear what you really say

To be attentive to your actions

    And to reply without delay


To give full notice to your feelings

To hold you when you're sad

To comfort you when in need

    And to scold you when you're bad


To accept the faults that you have

To love you as you're being

Is the complete union of happiness

    And a trust without seeing


To love you completely

To adore you without mar

Gives me all that I'll ever need

    With you as my shining star.

## A Marriage

For that as a ship on the ocean

       With a love that's as free as the breeze

A caring with warmth and compassion

       Is the true love that I give to thee.


To reason with true caring motives

       To see what is needed when in need

To give all that can really be given

       Is that of a love without greed.


The marriage of truth that we have

       The unit of one that we are

Gives strength to carry us onward

       With a love that will never be marred.

## A Baby's First Christmas

I see the tree, I see the lights,

But what is this I see tonight?

Why the glitter, why the glow?

There's something special here, I know!


The star on the treetop shining bright!

Must mean good, for I feel no fright.

Why the presents, why the toys?

Whatever it is, I still feel joy.


I feel the love, I see the smiles!

I see the cookies heaped in a pie.

My stockings are hung and filled I see.

Which means all the goodies must be for me!


Whatever day that this must be,

Should happen all over for the world to see.

From day to day, and night to night

Let it continue in sheer delight!

## Christmas

The skies are bright with glitter
And the laughter of love appears.
The chimes are ringing worldwide
The birthday of Christ is near.

In a small village, away in a manger,
A new life of salvation begins.
To bring peace and joyous contentment
To all that will worship Him.

He was sent by God, Our Almighty,
To give strength and love to all.
To caress and give warmness
To all that shall hear His call.

Raise up and give your thanks,
For a blessing so rich and pure.
On this blessed day of Christmas
For a love that will forever endure.

## Christmas Countdown

The countdown is here
>And Santa is near

With only four days to go
>The wreaths are all hung

And the caroling begun
>Knowing Christmas will be here soon.

Three days to go before all shall glow
>On the tree with the glitter so bright

The chimney needs sweeping, the cookies need keeping
>As we wait for that special night.

Two days to wait, for that important date
>For a holiday of love begins

Where bells will ring while children sing
>In thanks of what Santa brings.

One day remaining, and all are restraining

From eating plum pudding too early

For the Christmas cheer, is so very near

The impatience is too much, most surely.


Christmas is here, look at the cheer

Of the faces aglow with love

To give thanks and rejoice, with no other choice

Than to wish a Merry Christmas to all from

above.

## To My Lover

As the night hours draw near
I feel an emptiness within,
Knowing you're in the arms of another,
and realizing by paper, she wins.

Though we're wed not to one another,
changes nothing that I feel.
For my heart belongs only to you
and I know that this is real.

There is more to love than a contract
and living under one roof.
There must be an understanding
with no questions and no proof.

There must be a sharing of emotions
and this I have with you.
Even though she has your name,
in my heart I have said, "I do."

For we're wed by the ties that bind,
not by a written law.
For we have more than most have together
and a true love without a flaw.

I'll be yours forever and a day
with no doubt upon my mind
of the feelings of love you have for me
and no contract we've had to sign.

## A Free Spirit

Look the other way as I walk by
For I'm not the one to choose
My life is too confusing,
By winning me, you would lose.


I've much too many whims and fancies
Which you could only find upsetting
Why cause yourself the anguish?
By worries, tears and fretting?


For my life will take me to many lands
To many others that need fulfilling
Whether by love, need or curiosity
Where I'm needed, I am willing.


I can share certain parts of me,
But never can I give my all.
For my life has already been destined,
I must go wherever I'm called.

I'm a drifter as the clouds are across the sky

With the intent of love for others.

For each person whom I touch for just a minute

Becomes as close as though my brother.

## A Mother's Love

I wish I could dry the tears from your eyes
And mend your broken heart
And heal the wounds of a tortured soul
So you'll not feel torn apart.

All I can give you is a genuine love
From the depths of my old meager soul
And pray that God will give you strength
To reach your ultimate goal.

Life's path is not an easy one
Nor should be tread alone
Let me guide you, little one,
So your heart is not turn to stone.

For love is a gift from the heavens above
To be shared without undo question
Accept it as will no matter the pain
For the answer will soon be mentioned.

Trust enough in the great powers of God
To lead you through the tests of life
And I'll always be there to hold your hand
No matter how deep the strife.

For my love as your mother is deeper than all
And I'll always be by your side
To love you no matter what you do
To protect you, heal you and guide.

## Growth

An answer of love,

A destiny of reasoning.

A feeling of contentment,

Is all for achieving.


To know beauty and wisdom,

Of each passing day.

Brings the growth of our being,

In each and every way.

## I Guess What Will Be, Will Be

To live in a world of sadness
Seems so unfair to me.
But, I can see no real happiness.
I guess what will be, will be.

The earth below my wearied feet
Seems so shaky and weak to me
Or am I only imagining?
I guess what will be, will be.

I see sickness, hurt and pain
Murders, deaths and divorce decrees
To the point of complete discouragement.
I guess what will be, will be.

The misery, whining and complaining
The self-pity with so much glee
Has made me doubt the reason for living.
I guess what will be, will be.

But, I suppose there must be a reason

For the misery that seems to be

The most important part of a person's life.

I guess what will be, will be.

# Life Has No Guarantee

When you purchase items from a store,

In most cases proper you receive

Giving you a chance to repair if broken

The item with a guarantee.


You'll receive papers when your child is born,

Showing date and time and name,

But you're never given an option to return

If you're not satisfied with this game.


The responsibility is yours to keep,

To this life with love and glee,

No matter how many bad times there are,

Life has no guarantees.


No one said this job was easy,

To raise a child to an adult.

No one said you're always to be right,

That would merely be an insult.

But you do the best you can,

And let be what will be,

For you knew before you started,

Life has no guarantees.

## Prerequisites of a President

Presidents' strength should be outstanding
With a temperament to hold control
Of a nation who needs his guidance
To help fulfill their goals.

A Presidents' wisdom to make decisions
With a conscience of nothing to hide
Is a leader we all could trust throughout
Knowing to us he's never lied.

A Presidents' knowledge of human behavior
Should be more than from what he's read.
Common sense with intuitive emotions
And listen to what is said.

A Presidents' love for his fellow man
Should be true and not demanding.
And handled with the balance of God
And compassion and understanding.

A Presidents' honor should shine as bright
As the stars glisten in the night.
With a brilliance glow for all to see
So we'll never feel darkened fright.

A Presidents' guidance should be concern
For his people who truly believe
And trusted enough to guide them?
With dignity no one to deceive.

A Presidents' leadership for the people
Should be his concern every day.
So all the world can look with envy
Wishing they lived in the USA.

## The Day America Froze

Dear God, the horror we felt today
With sadness beyond all thoughts.
For those who suffered from the dastardly deeds
Of those who have no soul.

The fires roared, the screams poured out
With hopes that it all could end.
Yet, the fires rage within our hearts
With a path we all must to mend.

We helped so many throughout the times,
And this is what we get?
Families and friends who have lost their lives
From those who will feel no regret...

Yes, America froze for just one day
With effects that will ripple for years.
But the strength of our nation will never die
No matter how hard they try.

This is the time for all to stand strong
Prove who we really are.
Reach out to help your fellow man
Even though we'll have many scars.

Show the bastards, whoever they are
That America will not stand by
And watch our nation crumble in fear
No matter how others may try

September 11, 2001

## The Gypsy

One night the gypsy told me
Of a man who had eyes of blue
Would sweep me off my stable feet
But he'd never remain true.

She also told me he'd break my heart
As he's done with others in the past
She said I'd cry every night
Over this love that wouldn't last.

"Come on old gypsy woman," I said
"Stop telling me your crazy tales,
Just because you're not happy and all alone
Doesn't mean my true love will fail,"

I looked into her dark brown eyes
And this is what I said,
"Gypsy woman, you're the fool,
Go home and go to bed!"

As the years have passed and I lay in my bed
With pillows soaked of tears
I remember back to the gypsy's words
That were true throughout the years.


When I dreamt last night of the gypsy
She looked into my dark brown eyes and said,
"Now you're the fool, you know it all,
Go home and go to bed!"

## To Succeed

What is achievement?

Why must I succeed?

Where will it take me?

Whom will I need?


Will there be a tomorrow?

As there is today?

Will there be someone close

To show me the way?


But, the answer is love

A destiny of reasoning

A feeling of contentment

Is all for achieving.


To know beauty and wisdom

Of each passing day

Brings growth of our being

in every which way.

There is always a tomorrow
In spirit or mind
There is always the guidance
If we choose it to find.

## To Our President

A man with the power of a nation,

With the laws of man in his hands.

To be firm with love and compassion,

No matter which reason for which he stands.


To feel the feelings of all people's needs,

To know their emotions in all their deeds.

To give strength where weaknesses prevails,

No matter what else appears to fail.


To stand tall even when you are weak,

To hide emotions in what you must seek.

To be a man of wisdom and God,

To follow a path that is hard to trod.


To launch a hand of friendship to those who care
less,

To take ridicule and laughter and shrug off to your
best.

To know hatred by others with contempt in their
heart,

But to continue your duty and still do your part.

America is still beautiful and shall always be,
Forever and however the eyes may see.
Stand strong and brave, feel love and free,
Guide and protect us however you need.

## Wedding Song

Love is caring for each other's life
With never a question to ask
Of sincerity and true devotion
Nor hiding behind a mask.

To trust and believe with no doubt in mind
Of your partner's true love for you
Is to know the bonds and wondrous love
On this day as I say, "I do."

Standing beside you as we become one
Shows a light with a radiant glow
With respect and honor and our hearts held high
And for all the world to know.

For now I'm your mate till the end of time
To share in the good times and bad
To give you the strength that's needed through all
No matter how happy or sad.

Made in the USA
Middletown, DE
07 November 2015